THE DASH BETWEEN US

poems by

Cathy Porter

Finishing Line Press
Georgetown, Kentucky

THE DASH BETWEEN US

Copyright © 2022 by Cathy Porter
ISBN 978-1-64662-754-7 First Edition
All rights reserved under International and Pan-American Copyright Conventions. No part of this book may be reproduced in any manner whatsoever without written permission from the publisher, except in the case of brief quotations embodied in critical articles and reviews.

ACKNOWLEDGMENTS

The House Nobody Claims—*Pennine Ink*, UK
Ten Minutes In—*Willow Review*, College of Lake County
How To Rewrite Grief—*Green Hills Literary Lantern*, Truman State University
Not A Test—Forthcoming in *Art: Mag*
Will Brown, 1919—*The Haight Ashbury Literary Journal*
Holly, Who Works Overnights At The Kwik Shop—*Plainsongs*, Hastings College
There Goes My Hero—*Trajectory*
Screen Door Town—*The Avalon Literary Review*
Are We Great Yet?—*Poetry X Hunger*, Online
Vonnie, The Waffle House Waitress—*Pennine Ink*, UK
Run And Duck—*Amulet Poetry Magazine* (forthcoming in *misfit*, online)
No Sugar Tonight—*Nerve Cowboy*

Publisher: Leah Huete de Maines
Editor: Christen Kincaid
Cover Art: Cathy Porter
Author Photo: Cathy Porter
Cover Design: Elizabeth Maines McCleavy

Order online: www.finishinglinepress.com
also available on amazon.com

Author inquiries and mail orders:
Finishing Line Press
PO Box 1626
Georgetown, Kentucky 40324
USA

Table of Contents

Breonna 1

At The Foot 2

The House Nobody Claims 3

Ten Minutes In 4

Rings of Saturn 5

Inclusion 6

How to Rewrite Grief 7

All Of It 8

Not A Test 9

Will Brown, 1919 10

Holly, Who Works Overnights At The Kwik Shop 11

There Goes My Hero 12

Screen Door Town 13

65 Cents 14

Are We Great Yet? 15

Vonnie, The Waffle House Waitress 16

Run And Duck 17

Prince Always Knew 18

Behind The Shades 19

No Sugar Tonight 20

The Root 21

My Name Is Equality 22

BREONNA

We're told to keep calm
when injustice rears its ugly fist,
in a hail of bullets—

and every conclusion is another
punch. The view never changes,

but names and locations vary;
geography for the masses.

It's autumn; leaves turn as we turn
to the streets. This pain never goes
on hiatus.

Souls crushed in background noise.
People are tired, and not everybody
can get back up.

AT THE FOOT

Tonight, I have all the feelings
we try to stuff—the ones we
try to pray away—

as ghosts hang from the ceiling,
daring me to continue.

These days are feral, relief
on standby. This house makes
me squint

for a better look. We fall up
the stairs, lay down
at the foot.

Arrows trip from the sky;
rain moves in. Wet tears behind
the shades. Autumn winds
have passed us by.

THE HOUSE NOBODY CLAIMS

At the end of the block, it slumps—
like a sullen teenager stuck watching
a kid sister at a family wedding, or

the last kid picked for the team—
unwanted and unskilled; called on
only to fill a quota.

Chipped paint siding; a roof sure to
collapse with the next hail storm,
an old widow—

alone and scared, empty inside;
the lone green apple in a bushel of reds.
No lights, no phone, no story—
just time and nothing to kill.

TEN MINUTES IN

the conversation, he tells me
his name is Steven, apologizes
for cutting in front of me in line
at the coffee shop. He casually
mentions bullets he took to
the pelvic area in Iraq that's left
him with a bad limp, not to mention
memory issues.

"The only thing I was ever good at
was being a soldier."

Night terrors and isolation.
Shrink says he needs to get out and
meet people, but he's an introvert—
he's looking at photography
classes at the local community college.
"I need to get something going
in my life. I'm only 34 years old."

I let him talk, even when that talk
is disjointed and confusing.
He shakes my hand: "have to get back
to my apartment. Nice talking to you.
Don't forget my name."

RINGS OF SATURN

Corners drift apart
Days crush bones into dust
Animal clouds

I walk into buildings
Skin on skin, eyes burn
Behind open doorways

Men wait for guards to fall
Stray dogs roam, wild-eyed
Sirens circle the block

Explode into spaces
The body waits
Swallow bullets

Pause to reload
Pass fire between friends
All others deny

Corners drift apart
I walk into buildings
Alone

INCLUSION

On nights when I lose myself,
I watch for signs of you, visions
that push me through darkness.
The city on fire outside my window—
I remember your words of
inclusion, how to walk in stride
with others. You saw color and rejoiced—
and damn the ones who didn't get it.
Our world cries hard; the ugly
cry we all do, mostly alone.
I can see you sitting at the kitchen
table, holding court and setting
anybody straight who didn't
get on board: in this house, all
are welcome. Eyes like steel,
no fist needed.

HOW TO REWRITE GRIEF

Start with the word itself—
scatter the letters over the floor,

twist them in knots not even
a boy scout could undo, or—

pretend they're good luck pieces;
carry them in your pockets,

show them off on special
occasions, rub as needed—

admire the crooked back of 'G'—
the rigidity of 'I' between comrades,

give fist-bumps, group hugs;
resist the urge to bust them

all in the face—a hit as powerful
as the day your territory was invaded,

and time became another
word that needed a re-write.

ALL OF IT

Winter skin crawls into spring;
bones unthaw. Time will have to work
magic. Winds scatter debris
through yards and driveways—

Each gust a moment of nostalgia—
but some days are harder than others.
The streets are filled with sand.
A spring snowstorm is headed our way.

Years of twisted dreams, unraveled.
We'll fight as long as breath allows.
And when we rest, we'll know—
our days, we made count.

NOT A TEST

so
here
we
are

layers of desperation
drunk
under duress

old republics
re-opened

behind the eyes
cities
twisted
abandoned
high alert
high stress

watches
warnings
constant
connection
infection

the earth
cannot
continue
to
cover
for
us

WILL BROWN, 1919

We found your grave today—
Potter's Field, with 300 plus,
late autumn leaves a somber
altar—our dog statue-still
at the front. Old newspaper clips
capture the sick delight of the crowd—
children laughing as your body
(charred, because the bastards
weren't satisfied with a simple
hanging) is dragged through
the streets; the mayor trying
to restore order, barely escaping
his own lynching. The courthouse
set on fire. Thousands foaming like
rabid dogs. No evidence. Zilch.
100 years to get a proper marker.
Those ugly, laughing faces. We
left at dusk, as the sky poured
buckets—the drive home, quiet.
Even the dog whined.

HOLLY, WHO WORKS OVERNIGHTS AT THE KWIK SHOP

she's robbed -twice- between midnight and 5am
42 dollars and some change
thought she'd never see her son again
or her disabled mom
the cops keep her for hours
same questions over and over
she just wants to get home
see her son before school
they finally let her go
Rhonda is her shift relief—
gives her the report, tells her to be careful
be back at 11pm for her shift
hope it's just the usual crowd
for beer and smokes
or that one guy who hangs outside
smokes weed by the air pumps
keeps an eye on the place
gives her the good stuff
to get her through the night

THERE GOES MY HERO

Eddie's been hitting the booze and weed
non-stop since coming home.
But he's a hero; the whole town lets
him know it.

"Welcome Home Eddie!" banners everywhere:
the Mini-Mart, Ray's Tavern, the Church
of Christ.

Eddie doesn't want anyone to know;
he's no hero. Others did so much more—
others died.

The night-time panic attacks—the bombs that
go off in his brain. The endless shakes.
No off button.

He fought and fought hard. Made a few
friends, but lost track of them
after discharge.

The whole town slaps his back:
"bet you took out a bunch of 'em, huh?"

Eddie smiles, says how glad he is to be home.
Knocks back a beer, toasts Uncle Sam,
salutes the flag. Disappears when the
sun goes down.

SCREEN DOOR TOWN

The moon appears
in the red of swollen eyes.
These streets pound hard
at night.

And danger falls out of cars
on summer nights in heat.

Dad comes home with a stranger—
mom passed out on the couch.
The neighbors talk at church,
drink rumors at the bar.

The beat-up guitar behind
the bed collects dust;
a hollow body with open wounds.

Dad used to play—
but life went out-of-tune.
A pyramid of cans on the table;
nobody hiring. Even the radio
doesn't work.

65 CENTS

the sun rocks us to sleep
as the city comes to life

blankets over windows
the switch torn off the wall

one cigarette left
we'll fight over it later—

give this bed a good shake
pretend it's all good
down there

howling in the distance
the gallery calls
fun turned feral

65 cents on the table
stones and dates

the dash between us
the real story

ARE WE GREAT YET?

My neighbor's dog jumped his fence
the other day and took off running.

Across the city, on the west side,
the neighbors are shocked that a string
of cars have been broken into:

"This just doesn't happen here!"

These winter months bring out
the cold in too many hearts. Sends people
to the streets in acts of desperation.

Sara and Scott were kicked out of the bar
for pissing in each other's drinks.
Just like the government.

They still haven't found my neighbor's dog.
He was last seen trying to jump over
a higher fence down the road—
probably to get inside a warm house
for a bite to eat.

I don't know his name, but it doesn't matter—
nothing does, when you're scared and hungry.

VONNIE, THE WAFFLE HOUSE WAITRESS

in her early 60's
she slings it up
by choice or none
no shame in either
never forgets a name or face
gets the shaft on tips
but keeps that smile
like she knows something
you don't
works the room
like a rock star
on a farewell tour
stops a dine-and-dasher
with one arm
tops off my coffee
with the other
Journey on the jukebox
leads the crowd
in don't stop believin'
a drunken karaoke
with all the right words

RUN AND DUCK

History stutters before repetition—
we ignore the clues, through
decades and centuries. Tonight,
we're hit hard, the unknown our
familiar enemy; old paint, chipped
beyond repair. Health and wealth
make this difficult, my eyes wide-open
for the hammer. The news—one
more body-blow for bodies that
have absorbed too much, at the
expense of inequality; family and
friends, ghosted. Most duck when
shots are fired; we run first, then
duck. Both carry consequences.

PRINCE ALWAYS KNEW

The fields yawn and stretch;
morning fog rises to bless my windshield.
15 over the speed limit, not a cop in sight.
Radio static, followed by preaching.
It is Sunday, after all.

This damn virus makes for a short trip;
no snacks or bathroom breaks—
can't take the chance. Just enough gas
for a short cruise, to poke at monotony.

Days smear hope with anger—
the mind wanders into areas that haven't
been safe in years. Keep driving.

I think of you back home—
you told me to go by myself, get
out of the house; stay safe.

Up next on the playlist: Let's Go Crazy.
Prince always knew before
the rest of us.

BEHIND THE SHADES

Words hold power to uplift or scare

We drown them out
with any crutch we can find

Tonight's the night your eyes tell me
you want to say more

And my heart has hoarded clues
for months

How did our stars disappear so fast—

How did time become
one more thing we lost?

NO SUGAR TONIGHT

She slams a beer at the end
of the bar, does her best Def Leppard
air-guitar. Tells the guy next to
her about the night she spent
on their tour bus in '83, before
the drummer lost his arm—but
thinks they sold out for hair-metal
glory with Hysteria. Hates that "sugar
song", wishes Rick still had that arm.
More beer more talk more air-guitar—
but the dude is long gone, maybe
in the bathroom hiding, or headed
home to his wife, dog, 10 cats.
Just a small-town girl, livin' in a
lonely world—no trains going
anywhere, not even with
a different band.

THE ROOT

If we bleed truth, facts will
Challenge past illusions.

This new motion—sparks fly off
Skin, voices compete with the tallest

Mountain. Our ghosts are proud,
And feet pound. We would not

Go away, and we won't. Inclement
Weather—tuck and roll, the push is in

The pull. When asked why, speak eye
Level. Speak heart. Speak tongue for

The ones that belong to silence. Speak
Strength for the ones who are too

Weak to lift themselves to be fed.
And when words fail to breathe—

Rest easy and know the fight no
Longer belongs to the ones who

Look down from the rooftops.

MY NAME IS EQUALITY

And I have been forgotten.
Everybody says they want me—but not
many have my back.

You may think you've seen me around
at times—it's probably just my shadow.
I tend to drift.

I get left outside on the coldest
of nights. I get ignored in the heat.

Sometimes, I get so mad, I run the streets
and try to get someone—anyone—
to listen to me.

My anger can explode. A knee on the neck
will do that.

I'm exhausted, but I can never sleep.
Most of my friends are gone.

My patience is depleted. I have walked
for miles. My shoes are gone.
Time is gone.

My seat at the table is long overdue.
It's time to eat.

Most of my friends are gone.

I can't breathe. We can't breathe.
A knee on the neck: 8:46.

Cathy Porter has been writing poetry and short stories since high school. She began submitting her work to journals in 2000, and hasn't stopped since. Writing has been a therapeutic tool to help cope with the many curve balls of life. Her self-published chapbook, *Taking In Strays,* appeared in 2006; Northern Stars published *Scattered Rainbows* in 2007. Recent poems and short stories have appeared in *Trajectory, Conceit Magazine, Amulet, Bear Creek Haiku, The Haight Ashbury Literary Journal, Fine Lines, Nerve Cowboy, Time Of Singing,* and *Talking River Review.* Along with her three chapbooks from Finishing Line Press, Cathy has chapbooks available from Dancing Girl Press and Maverick Duck Press. She has been nominated for several Pushcart Prizes. Cathy is currently working on a full-length poetry collection, as well as a novel and short-story collection. She lives in Omaha, Nebraska with her husband Lenny, their dog Marley, and cats Cody and Mini. She encourages people to contact her at cathleenp9495@gmail.com.

www.ingramcontent.com/pod-product-compliance
Lightning Source LLC
LaVergne TN
LVHW041524070426
835507LV00012B/1805